PIANO
VOCAL
GUITAR

HAL LEONARD
COUNTRY
DECADE SERIES

THE **2000s**

35

GREAT
SONGS

FROM
COUNTRY'S
GREATEST
STARS

BREATHE
FAITH HILL
ALCOHOL
BRAD PAISLEY
BEER FOR MY HORSES
TOBY KEITH

ISBN 1-4234-0573-0

HAL•LEONARD®
CORPORATION

7777 W. BLUEMOUND RD. P.O. BOX 13819 MILWAUKEE, WI 53213

Visit Hal Leonard Online at
www.halleonard.com

CONTENTS

Page	Song	Artist	Peak Chart Position	Year
4	Alcohol	Brad Paisley	4	2005
11	American Soldier	Toby Keith	1	2004
18	Angry All the Time	Tim McGraw	1	2001
27	Beer for My Horses	Toby Keith	1	2003
34	The Best Day	George Strait	1	2000
40	Best of Intentions	Travis Tritt	1	2000
46	Bless the Broken Road	Rascal Flatts	1	2005
53	Blessed	Martina McBride	1	2002
62	Born to Fly	Sara Evans	1	2001
70	Breathe	Faith Hill	1	2000
76	Buy Me a Rose	Kenny Rogers with Alison Krauss & Billy Dean	1	2000
88	Cowboy Take Me Away	Dixie Chicks	1	2000
96	Have You Forgotten?	Darryl Worley	1	2003
81	Help Pour Out the Rain (Lacey's Song)	Buddy Jewell	3	2003
102	I Am a Man of Constant Sorrow	The Soggy Bottom Boys	35	2002
110	I Hope You Dance	Lee Ann Womack with Sons Of The Desert	1	2000
118	I Love This Bar	Toby Keith	1	2003

Page	Song	Artist	Peak Chart Position	Year
105	I Miss My Friend	Darryl Worley	1	2002
124	I'm Already There	Lonestar	1	2001
132	I'm Gonna Miss Her (The Fishin' Song)	Brad Paisley	1	2002
136	Landslide	Dixie Chicks	2	2002
152	Long Black Train	Josh Turner	13	2004
158	My Best Friend	Tim McGraw	1	2000
164	No Shoes No Shirt (No Problems)	Kenny Chesney	2	2003
170	One More Day (With You)	Diamond Rio	1	2001
176	Only in America	Brooks & Dunn	1	2001
145	Redneck Woman	Gretchen Wilson	1	2004
184	Remember When	Alan Jackson	1	2004
190	Three Wooden Crosses	Randy Travis	1	2003
196	The Way You Love Me	Faith Hill	1	2000
200	What I Really Meant to Say	Cyndi Thomson	1	2001
206	Where the Stars and Stripes and the Eagle Fly	Aaron Tippin	2	2002
214	Where Were You (When the World Stopped Turning)	Alan Jackson	1	2001
222	Who I Am	Jessica Andrews	1	2001
229	You'll Think of Me	Keith Urban	1	2004

ALCOHOL

Words and Music by
BRAD PAISLEY

friends ___ or get you fired ___ from work.
drink or two that I can make you put that lamp-

shade on your head. And since the day I left ___ Mil-

wau - kee; Lynch - burg; Bor - deaux,

France; ___ been ___ mak - in' { the bars ___
                                  { a fool ___ out of

AMERICAN SOLDIER

Words and Music by TOBY KEITH
and CHUCK CANNON

I'm just try'n' to be a fa - ther, raise a daugh - ter and _ a son. _ Be a
do it for the mon - ey, there's _ bills that I _ can't pay. _ I don't

lov - er to _ their moth - er, ev - 'ry - thing to ev - 'ry - one. _ Up and
do it for _ the glo - ry, I just do it an - y - way. _ Pro -

at 'em bright _ and ear - ly, I'm all bus' - ness in _ my suit. Yeah, I'm
vid - ing for _ our fu - ture's my re - spon - si - bil - i - ty. Yeah, I'm

D.S. al Coda

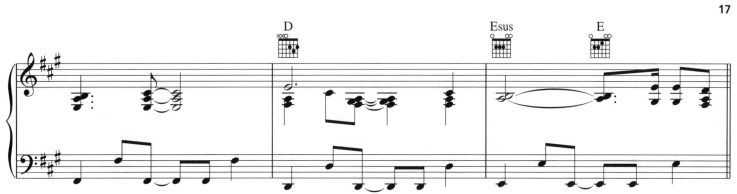

ANGRY ALL THE TIME

Words and Music by
BRUCE ROBISON

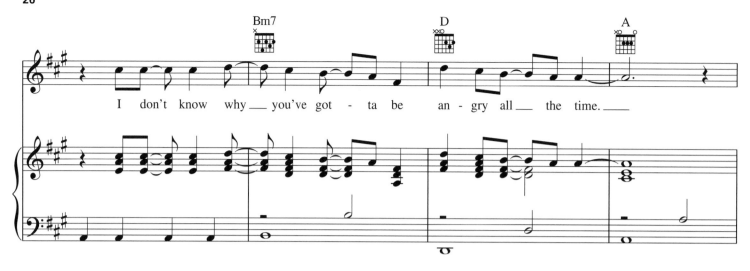

I don't know why ___ you've got - ta be an - gry all ___ the time. ___

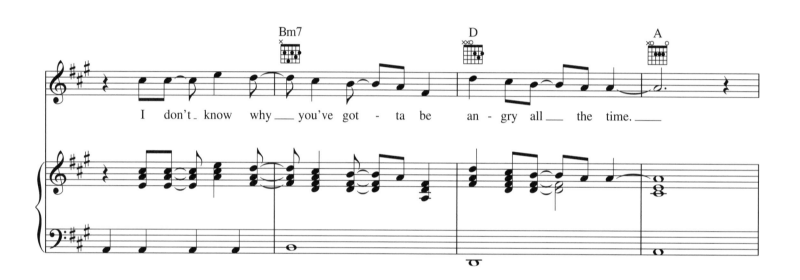

I don't ___ know why ___ you've got - ta be an - gry all ___ the time. ___

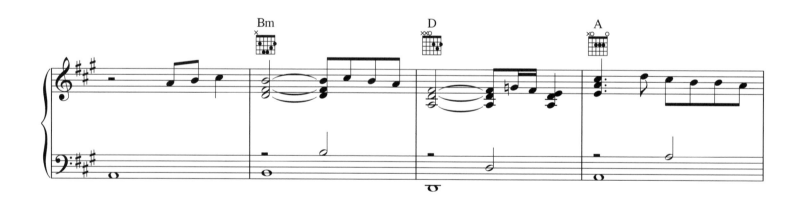

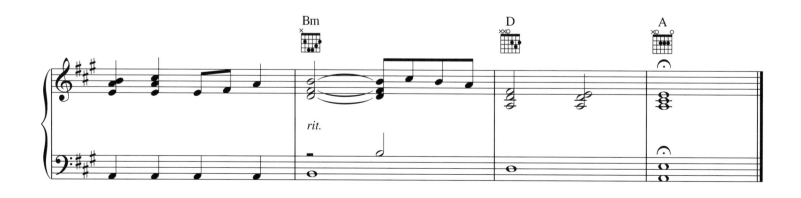

rit.

BEER FOR MY HORSES

Words and Music by TOBY KEITH
and SCOTT EMERICK

THE BEST DAY

Words and Music by DEAN DILLON
and CARSON CHAMBERLAIN

We load-ed up my old sta-tion wag-on with a
fif-teenth birth-day rolled a-round,

tent, a Cole-man and sleep-in' bags, some fish-in' poles, a
clas-sic cars were his thing. When I pulled in the drive with

cool-er of Cokes. Three days be-fore we had to be back. When you
that old Vette, I thought that boy would go in-sane. When you're

BEST OF INTENTIONS

Words and Music by
TRAVIS TRITT

BLESS THE BROKEN ROAD

Words and Music by MARCUS HUMMON,
BOBBY BOYD and JEFF HANNA

BLESSED

Words and Music by BRETT JAMES,
HILLARY LINDSEY and TROY VERGES

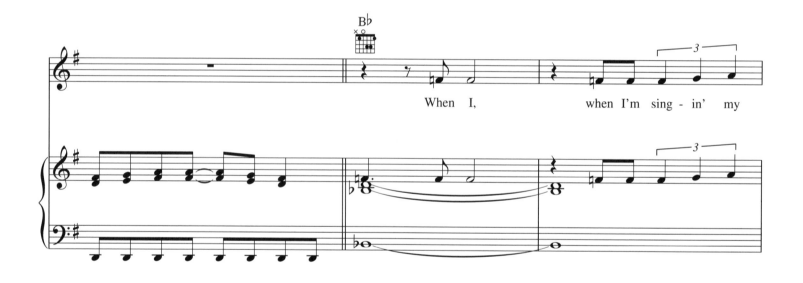

When I, when I'm sing - in' my

kids to sleep, when I feel you hold - in' me,

BORN TO FLY

Words and Music by SARA EVANS,
DARRELL SCOTT and MARCUS HUMMON

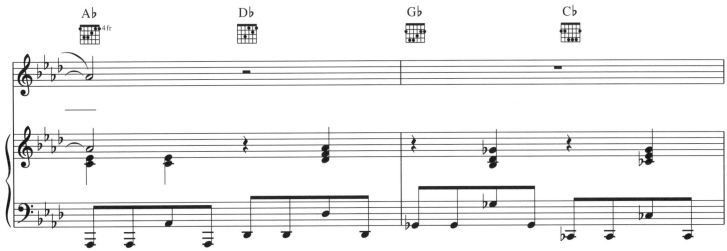

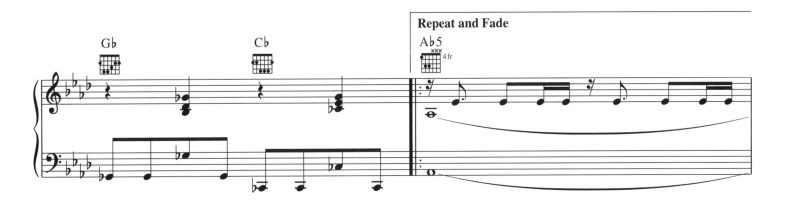

BREATHE

Words and Music by HOLLY LAMAR
and STEPHANIE BENTLEY

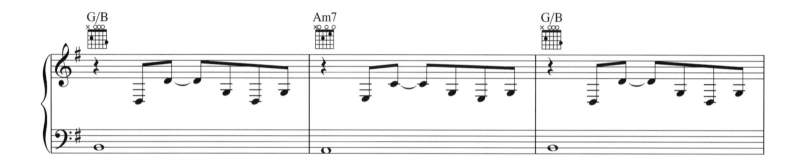

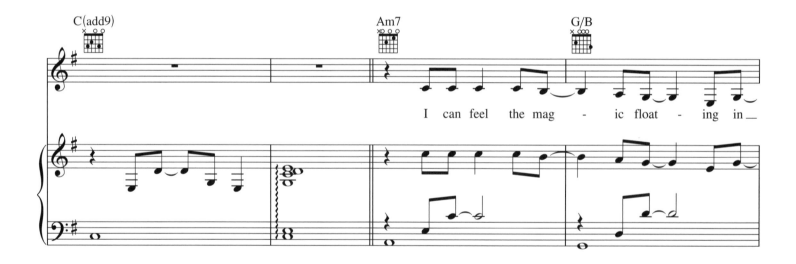

I can feel the mag - ic float - ing in the air.

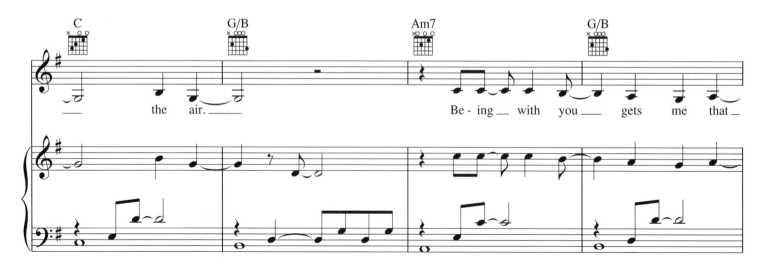

Be - ing with you gets me that

BUY ME A ROSE

Words and Music by ERIK HICKENLOOPER
and JIM FUNK

HELP POUR OUT THE RAIN
(Lacey's Song)

Words and Music by
BUDDY JEWELL

The mo-ment was _____ cus-tom-made to or-der: _____ I was rid-in' with _____ my daugh-

Well, I _____ won't lie. _____ I pulled that car right o-ver _____ and I sat _____ there on _____ the shoul-

COWBOY TAKE ME AWAY

Words and Music by MARCUS HUMMON
and MARTIE SEIDEL

Recorded a half step lower.

HAVE YOU FORGOTTEN?

Words and Music by DARRYL WORLEY
and WYNN VARBLE

Lyrics:
I hear peo-ple say-in' we don't need this war. _
They took all the foot-age off my T V. _

But I say there's some _ things worth fight-in' for.
Said it's too dis-turb-ing for you and me.

I AM A MAN OF CONSTANT SORROW

Words and Music by
CARTER STANLEY

sor - row._____ I've seen trou - ble all__ my
trou - ble,_____ no pleas - ure here_____ on earth I've
lov - er,_____ I nev - er ex - pect_____ to see__ you a -
val - ley_____ for man - y years_____ where I__ may lay,
stran - ger;_____ my face__ you nev - er will see__ no

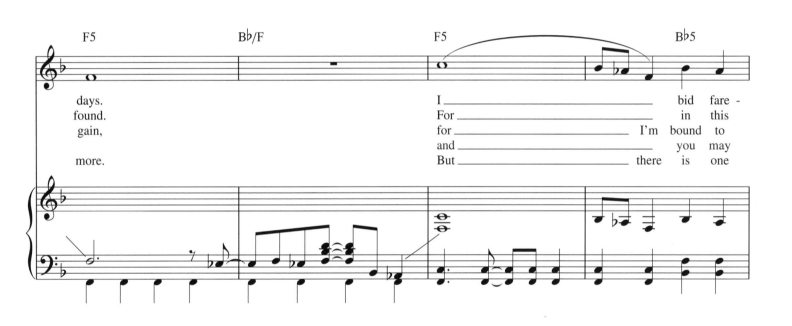

days. I_____ bid fare -
found. For_____ in this
gain, for_____ I'm bound to
more. and_____ you may
But_____ there is one

well_____ to old__ Ken - tuck - y,_____ the place_ where I____
world_____ I'm bound_ to ram - ble;_____ I have_ no friends____
ride_____ that North - ern rail - road;_____ per - haps_ I'll die____
learn_____ to love__ an - oth - er_____ while I__ am sleep -
prom - ise that is giv - en:_____ I'll meet_ you on____

was born and raised. The place where
to help me now. He has no
up - on this train. Per - haps he'll
ing in my grave. While he is
God's gold - en shore. He'll meet you

he _____ was born and raised.
friends _____ to help him now.
die _____ up - on this train.
sleep - ing in his grave.
on _____ God's gold - en

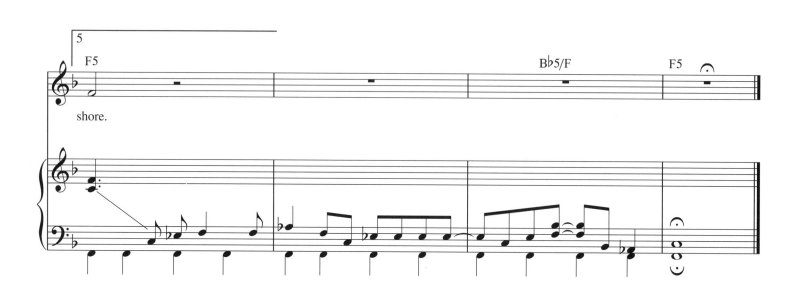

shore.

I MISS MY FRIEND

Words and Music by TOM SHAPIRO,
TONY MARTIN and MARK NESLER

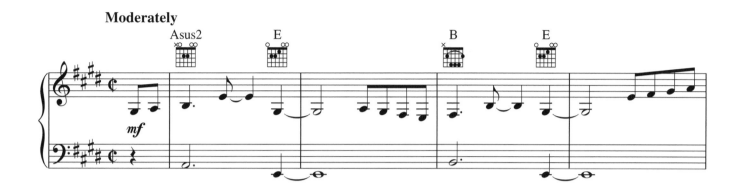

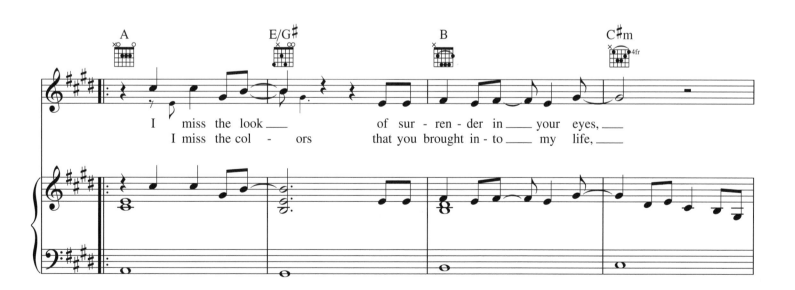

I miss the look ____ of sur - ren - der in ____ your eyes, ____
I miss the col - ors that you brought in - to ____ my life, ____

I HOPE YOU DANCE

Words and Music by TIA SILLERS
and MARK D. SANDERS

hope you nev - er lose _____ your sense of won - der.
nev - er fear ___ those ___ moun - tains in the dis - tance.

I LOVE THIS BAR

Words and Music by TOBY KEITH
and SCOTTY EMERICK

I'M ALREADY THERE

Words and Music by RICHIE McDONALD,
FRANK MYERS and GARY BAKER

called her on ___ the road ___ from a lone - ly, cold ___ ho - tel ___ room ___ just to

hear her say ___ "I love ___ you" one ___ more time. ___ And

I'M GONNA MISS HER
(The Fishin' Song)

Words and Music by BRAD PAISLEY
and FRANK ROGERS

LANDSLIDE

Words and Music by
STEVIE NICKS

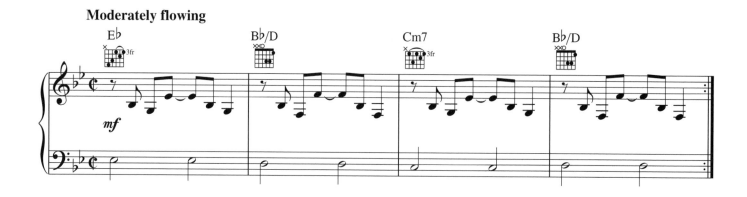

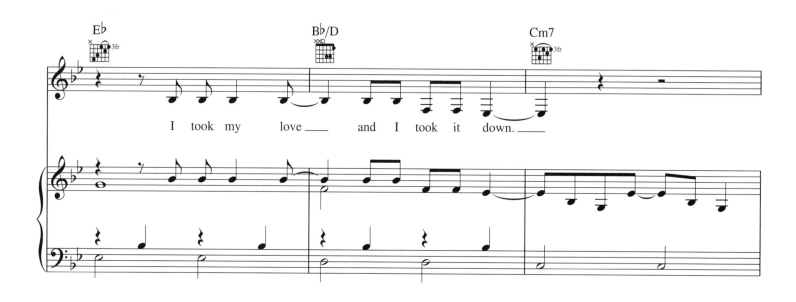

I took my love ___ and I took it down. ___

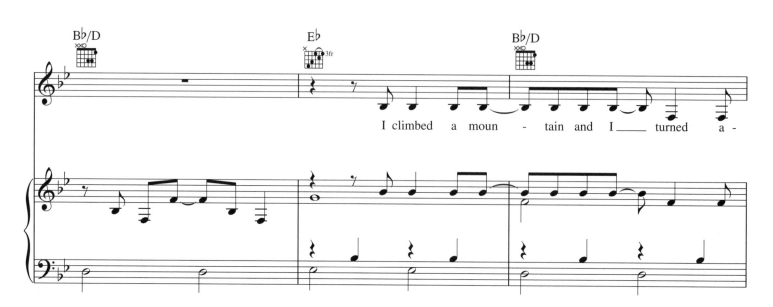

I climbed a moun - tain and I ___ turned a -

REDNECK WOMAN

Words and Music by GRETCHEN WILSON
and JOHN RICH

Recorded a half step lower.

yeah. ____ (Hell, yeah!)

Instrumental solo

I'm a red - neck wom - an, I ain't no

LONG BLACK TRAIN

Words and Music by
JOSH TURNER

MY BEST FRIEND

Words and Music by AIMEE MAYO
and BILL LUTHER

I nev-er had no one that I could count ___
You stand ___ by me and you be-lieve ___ in ___

___ on.   I've been let down ___ so man-y times. ___
___ me   like no-bod - y ev-er has. ___

NO SHOES NO SHIRT
(No Problems)

Words and Music by
CASEY BEATHARD

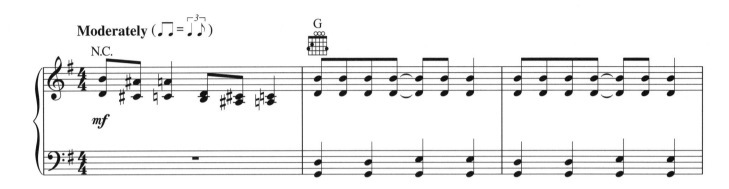

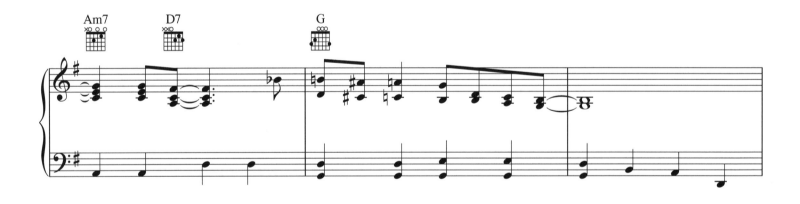

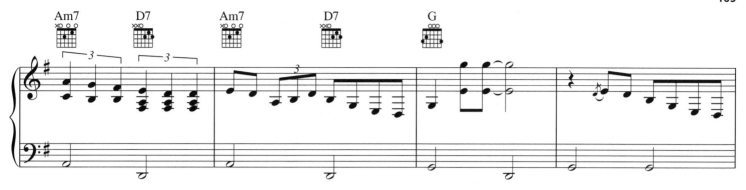

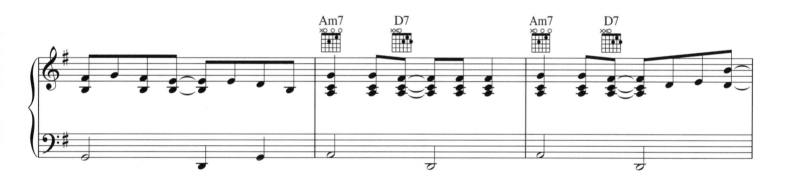

I've been up ____ to my neck ____ work-in' six ____
____ on a chair ____ and the sand ____

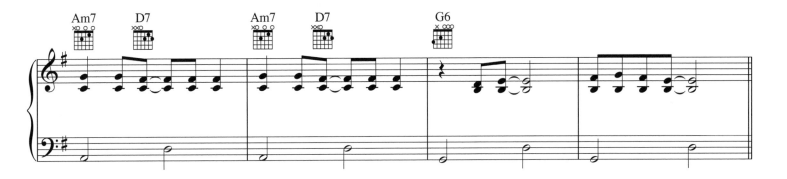

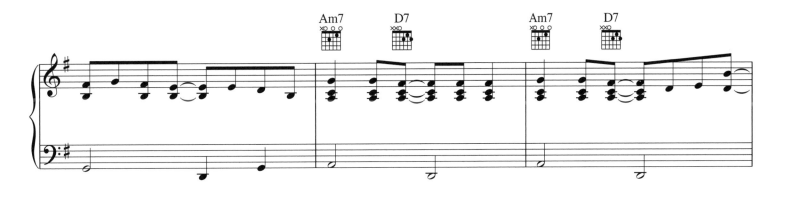

ONE MORE DAY

(With You)

Words and Music by STEVEN DALE JONES
and BOBBY TOMERLIN

ONLY IN AMERICA

Words and Music by KIX BROOKS,
DON COOK and RONNIE ROGERS

Moderately fast

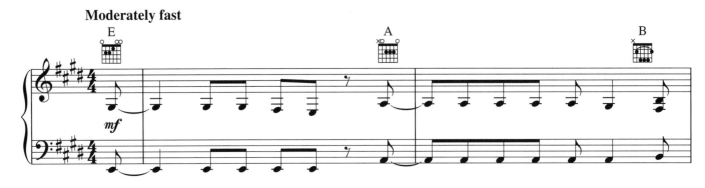

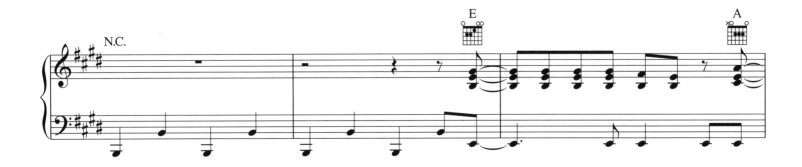

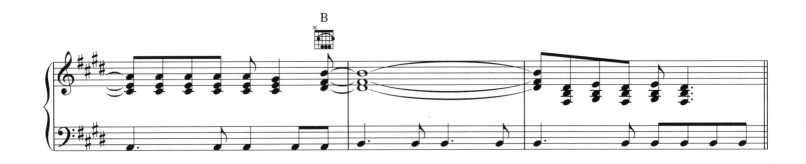

Sun com-in' up   o-ver New York Cit - y.
Sun go-in' down   on an L. A. free-way,

On -

REMEMBER WHEN

Words and Music by
ALAN JACKSON

Re-mem - ber when _____ the

we

THREE WOODEN CROSSES

Words and Music by KIM WILLIAMS
and DOUG JOHNSON

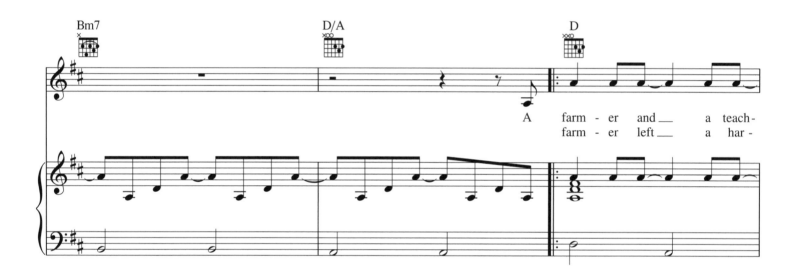

A farm- er and ___ a teach-
farm- er left ___ a har-

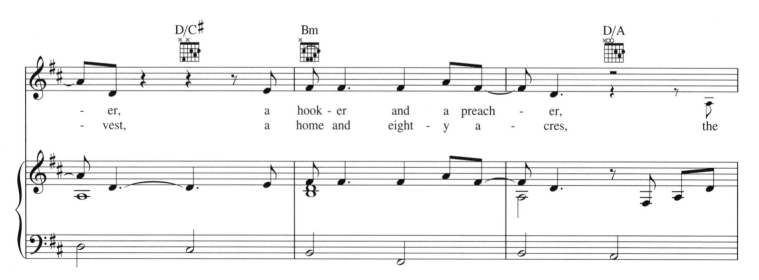

-er, a hook- er and a preach - er,
-vest, a home and eight- y a - cres, the

Recorded a half step lower.

THE WAY YOU LOVE ME

Words and Music by MICHAEL DULANEY
and KEITH FOLLESE

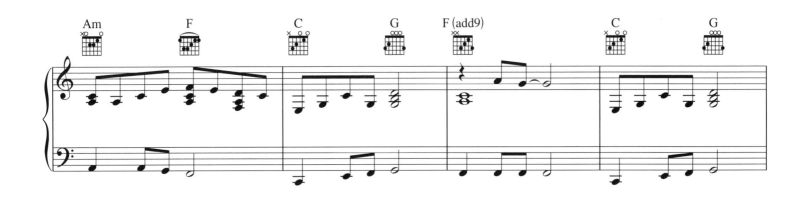

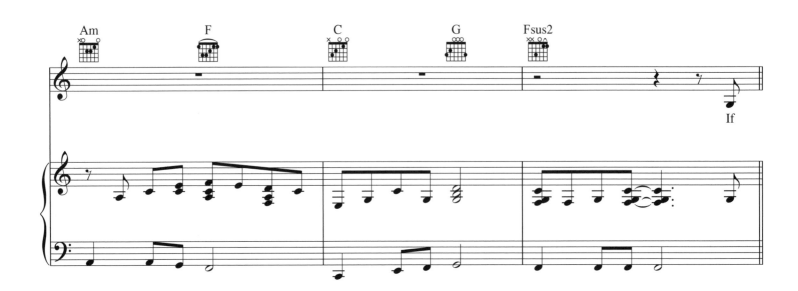

WHAT I REALLY MEANT TO SAY

Words and Music by CYNDI THOMSON,
CHRIS WATERS and TOMMY LEE JAMES

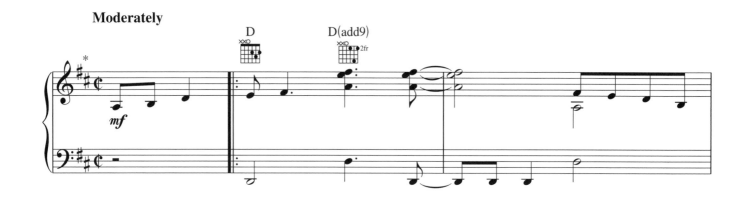

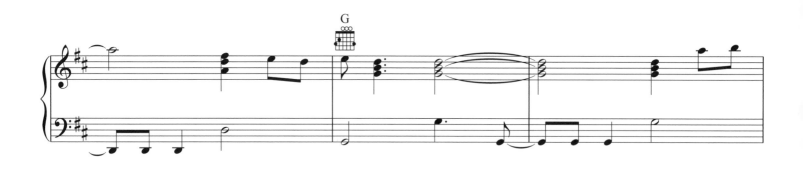

* Recorded a half lower.

night I have - n't cried. ___ And, ba - by, here's ___ the truth: ___

I'm still in love ___ with you, ___

yeah. That's what I real - ly meant ___ to say. ___

WHERE THE STARS AND STRIPES AND THE EAGLE FLY

Words and Music by AARON TIPPIN,
CASEY BEATHARD and KENNY BEARD

Well, if you ask me, where I___ come from,

here's what I___ tell ev-'ry-one.___

WHERE WERE YOU
(When the World Stopped Turning)

Words and Music by
ALAN JACKSON

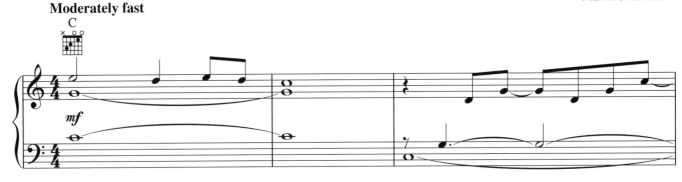

Where were you when the world ___ stopped turn-in'   that Sep - tem - ber

day?

{ Out in the yard ___ with your wife and chil - dren   or
{ Teach - in' a class ___ full of in - no - cent chil - dren   or

C N N,___ but I'm not___ sure I can tell you the dif - f'rence in I - raq and I -

ran. But I know Je - sus and I_____ talk to God___ and I re -

mem - ber this from when I was young: faith, hope and love are some

good things He gave us and the great - est is love.

WHO I AM

Words and Music by BRETT JAMES
and TROY VERGES

YOU'LL THINK OF ME

Words and Music by TY LACY,
DENNIS MATKOSKY and DARRELL BROWN

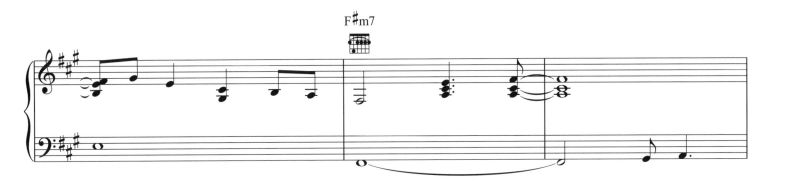

I woke up ear-
I went out driv-

but don't wor-ry, I'll be fine. I'm gon-na be al-right. While you're sleep-in' with your pride, wish-in' I could hold you tight, I'll be o-ver you and on with my life.

And you're gon - na think _ of me.

Contemporary & Classic Country

More great country hits from Hal Leonard arranged for piano and voice with guitar chords.

The Best Country Songs Ever – 2nd Edition

This outstanding collection features 78 country favorites: Always on My Mind • Blue • Crying • Daddy Sang Bass • Friends in Low Places • God Bless the U.S.A. • He Stopped Loving Her Today • I Fall to Pieces • King of the Road • Love Without End, Amen • Mammas Don't Let Your Babies Grow Up to Be Cowboys • Rhinestone Cowboy • Stand by Your Man • Wabash Cannonball • more.
00359135 ....$17.95

Country Gospel U.S.A.

Piano/guitar/4-part vocal arrangements of 50 well-known country/gospel songs: An American Trilogy • Daddy Sang Bass • I Saw the Light • Love Lifted Me • Mansion over the Hilltop • Turn Your Radio On • Will the Circle Be Unbroken.
00240139 ....$10.95

Country Legends

A budget-priced collection of 50 favorites from country music's finest. Includes: Blue Eyes Crying in the Rain • Down at the Twist and Shout • Help Me Make It Through the Night • I Fought the Law • Mountain Music • Tie a Yellow Ribbon Round the Ole Oak Tree • Walkin' After Midnight • You Are My Sunshine • Your Cheatin' Heart • and more.
00315339.......................................$12.95

Country Love Songs – 4th Edition

This edition features 34 romantic country favorites, including: Amazed • Breathe • For the Good Times • I Need You • The Keeper of the Stars • Love Can Build a Bridge • One Boy, One Girl • Stand by Me • This Kiss • Through the Years • Valentine • more.
00311528.......................................$14.95

Country Songs – Budget Book

You get a lot of bang for your buck with this great collection of 90 songs for only $12.95! Titles include: All My Ex's Live in Texas • Boot Scootin' Boogie • Cowboy Take Me Away • Elvira • Hey, Good Lookin' • Lucille • Okie from Muskogee • Sixteen Tons • and many more!
00310833.......................................$12.95

Country Standards
PIANO PLAY ALONG, VOLUME 6

Practice and perform with professional-sounding accompaniments on CD to match 8 songs in the book. Includes: Blue Eyes Crying in the Rain • Crazy • King of the Road • Oh, Lonesome Me • Ring of Fire • Tennessee Waltz • You Are My Sunshine • Your Cheatin' Heart.
00311077 Book/CD Pack $12.95

Good Ol' Country

58 old-time favorites: Candy Kisses • Cold, Cold Heart • Crazy • Crying in the Chapel • Deep in the Heart of Texas • Faded Love • Green Green Grass of Home • Hey, Good Lookin' • I Can't Stop Loving You • Sweet Dreams • Tennessee Waltz • You Are My Sunshine • You Don't Know Me • more.
00310517 ....$14.95

The Grand Ole Opry Songbook

80 songs from 80 years of country music are featured in this collection: Coal Miner's Daughter (Loretta Lynn) • Green Green Grass of Home (Porter Wagoner) • I Was Country When Country Wasn't Cool (Barbara Mandrell) • When You Say Nothing at All (Alison Krauss) • and more. Includes photos and articles.
00311248 ....$19.95

COUNTRY MUSIC TELEVISION'S
100 Greatest Songs of Country Music

In 2003, Country Music Television compiled a panel of experts to rank the 100 greatest country songs of all time. This folio presents all 100 songs: Crazy (#3) • Friends in Low Places (#6) • He Stopped Loving Her Today (#2) • Ring of Fire (#4) • Stand by Your Man (#1) • Your Cheatin' Heart (#5) • and many more.
00306544.......................................$29.95

COUNTRY MUSIC TELEVISION'S
100 Greatest Country Love Songs

This book provides an amazing collection of classic and contemporary country love songs as voted on by Country Music Television, including: Always on My Mind • Behind Closed Doors • Could I Have This Dance • Forever and Ever, Amen • I Fall to Pieces • Lady • Ring of Fire • Stand by Your Man • You're Still the One • and more.
00311159.......................................$24.95

100 Most Wanted

Highlights: A Boy Named Sue • Break It to Me Gently • Crying My Heart out over You • Heartbroke • I.O.U. • I Know a Heartache When I See One • Mammas Don't Let Your Babies Grow Up to Be Cowboys • My Heroes Have Always Been Cowboys • Stand by Me • Save the Last Dance for Me • You're the First Time I've Thought About Leaving • You're the Reason God Made Oklahoma • many more.
00360730.......................................$15.95

Top Country Hits of '04-'05

20 of the year's best from country's hottest stars: American Soldier • Back When • Days Go By • How Am I Doin' • In a Real Love • Long Black Train • Mr. Mom • Mud on the Tires • Nothin 'Bout Love Makes Sense • Party for Two • Redneck Woman • Stays in Mexico • This One's for the Girls • The Woman with You • more.
00311212 ....$14.95

20th Century Country Music

Over 70 country classics representative of a century's worth of music, including: All the Gold in California • Always on My Mind • Amazed • Blue Moon of Kentucky • Boot Scootin' Boogie • Breathe • Crazy • Friends in Low Places • Harper Valley P.T.A. • Hey, Good Lookin' • Ring of Fire • and more.
00310673.......................................$19.95

Wedding Songs Country Style – 2nd Edition

An excellent selection of 35 popular "country style" wedding and love songs. New, old and unique songs are featured. Includes: The Keeper of the Stars • Marry Me • Grow Old with Me • One Boy, One Girl • Vows Go Unbroken • When You Say Nothing at All • and many others.
00310183 ....$14.95

FOR MORE INFORMATION, SEE YOUR LOCAL MUSIC DEALER, OR WRITE TO:

7777 W. BLUEMOUND RD. P.O. BOX 13819 MILWAUKEE, WI 53213

Visit Hal Leonard online at **www.halleonard.com**

THE ULTIMATE SONGBOOKS

PIANO PLAY-ALONG

These great songbook/CD packs come with our standard arrangements for piano and voice with guitar chord frames plus a CD.
The CD includes a full performance of each song, as well as a second track without the piano part so you can play "lead" with the band!

Vol. 1 Movie Music
Come What May • Forrest Gump – Main Title (Feather Theme) • My Heart Will Go On (Love Theme from *Titanic*) • The Rainbow Connection • Tears in Heaven • A Time for Us • Up Where We Belong • Where Do I Begin (Love Theme).
00311072 P/V/G......................$12.95

Vol. 2 Jazz Ballads
Autumn in New York • Do You Know What It Means to Miss New Orleans • Georgia on My Mind • In a Sentimental Mood • More Than You Know • The Nearness of You • The Very Thought of You • When Sunny Gets Blue.
00311073 P/V/G......................$12.95

Vol. 3 Timeless Pop
Ebony and Ivory • Every Breath You Take • From a Distance • I Write the Songs • In My Room • Let It Be • Oh, Pretty Woman • We've Only Just Begun.
00311074 P/V/G......................$12.95

Vol. 4 Broadway Classics
Ain't Misbehavin' • Cabaret • If I Were a Bell • Memory • Oklahoma • Some Enchanted Evening • The Sound of Music • You'll Never Walk Alone.
00311075 P/V/G $12.95

Vol. 5 Disney
Beauty and the Beast • Can You Feel the Love Tonight • Colors of the Wind • Go the Distance • Look Through My Eyes • A Whole New World • You'll Be in My Heart • You've Got a Friend in Me.
00311076 P/V/G......................$12.95

Vol. 6 Country Standards
Blue Eyes Crying in the Rain • Crazy • King of the Road • Oh, Lonesome Me • Ring of Fire • Tennessee Waltz • You Are My Sunshine • Your Cheatin' Heart.
00311077 P/V/G $12.95

Vol. 7 Love Songs
Can't Help Falling in Love • (They Long to Be) Close to You • Here, There and Everywhere • How Deep Is Your Love • I Honestly Love You • Maybe I'm Amazed • Wonderful Tonight • You Are So Beautiful.
00311078 P/V/G......................$12.95

Vol. 8 Classical Themes
Can Can • Habanera • Humoresque • In the Hall of the Mountain King • Minuet in G Major • Piano Concerto No. 21 in C Major, 2nd Movement Excerpt • Prelude in E Minor, Op. 28, No. 4 • Symphony No. 5 in C Minor, 1st Movement Excerpt.
00311079 Piano Solo $12.95

Vol. 9 Children's Songs
Do-Re-Mi • It's a Small World • Linus and Lucy • Sesame Street Theme • Sing • Winnie the Pooh • Won't You Be My Neighbor? • Yellow Submarine.
0311080 P/V/G $12.95

Vol. 10 Wedding Classics
Air on the G String • Ave Maria • Bridal Chorus • Canon in D • Jesu, Joy of Man's Desiring • Ode to Joy • Trumpet Voluntary • Wedding March.
00311081 Piano Solo................$12.95

Vol. 11 Wedding Favorites
All I Ask of You • Don't Know Much • Endless Love • Grow Old with Me • In My Life • Longer • Wedding Processional • You and I.
00311097 P/V/G $12.95

Vol. 12 Christmas Favorites
Blue Christmas • The Christmas Song • Do You Hear What I Hear • Here Comes Santa Claus • I Saw Mommy Kissing Santa Claus • Let It Snow! Let It Snow! Let It Snow! • Merry Christmas, Darling • Silver Bells.
00311137 P/V/G $12.95

Vol. 13 Yuletide Favorites
Angels We Have Heard on High • Away in a Manger • Deck the Hall • The First Noel • Go, Tell It on the Mountain • Jingle Bells • Joy to the World • O Little Town of Bethlehem.
00311138 P/V/G......................$12.95

Vol. 14 Pop Ballads
Have I Told You Lately • I'll Be There for You • It's All Coming Back to Me Now • Looks Like We Made It • Rainy Days and Monday • Say You, Say Me • She's Got a Way • Your Song.
00311145 P/V/G......................$12.95

Vol. 15 Favorite Standards
Call Me • The Girl from Ipanema • Moon River • My Way • Satin Doll • Smoke Gets in Your Eyes • Strangers in the Night • The Way You Look Tonight.
00311146 P/V/G......................$12.95

Vol. 16 TV Classics
The Brady Bunch • Green Acres Theme • Happy Days • Johnny's Theme • Love Boat Theme • Mister Ed • The Munsters Theme • Where Everybody Knows Your Name.
00311147 P/V/G......................$12.95

Vol. 17 Movie Favorites
Back to the Future • Theme from E.T. • Footloose • For All We Know • Somewhere in Time • Somewhere Out There • Theme from *Terms of Endearment* • You Light Up My Life.
00311148 P/V/G......................$12.95

Vol. 18 Jazz Standards
All the Things You Are • Bluesette • Easy Living • I'll Remember April • Isn't It Romantic? • Stella by Starlight • Tangerine • Yesterdays.
00311149 P/V/G......................$12.95

Vol. 19 Contemporary Hits
Beautiful • Calling All Angels • Don't Know Why • If I Ain't Got You • 100 Years • This Love • A Thousand Miles • You Raise Me Up.
00311162 P/V/G......................$12.95

Vol. 20 R&B Ballads
After the Love Has Gone • All in Love Is Fair • Hello • I'll Be There • Let's Stay Together • Midnight Train to Georgia • Tell It like It Is • Three Times a Lady.
00311163 P/V/G......................$12.95

Vol. 21 Big Bands
All or Nothing at All • Apple Honey • April in Paris • Cherokee • In the Mood • Opus One • Stardust • Stompin' at the Savoy.
00311164 P/V/G......................$12.95

Vol. 22 Rock Classics
Against All Odds • Bennie and the Jets • Come Sail Away • Do It Again • Free Bird • Jump • Wanted Dead or Alive • We Are the Champions.
00311165 P/V/G......................$12.95

Vol. 23 Worship Classics
Awesome God • How Majestic Is Your Name • Lord, Be Glorified • Lord, I Lift Your Name on High • Praise the Name of Jesus • Shine, Jesus, Shine • Step by Step • There Is a Redeemer.
00311166 P/V/G......................$12.95

Vol. 24 Les Misérables
Bring Him Home • Castle on a Cloud • Do You Hear the People Sing? • Drink with Me • Empty Chairs at Empty Tables • I Dreamed a Dream • A Little Fall of Rain • On My Own.
00311169 P/V/G......................$12.95

Vol. 25 The Sound of Music
Climb Ev'ry Mountain • Do-Re-Mi • Edelweiss • Maria • My Favorite Things • Sixteen Going on Seventeen • Something Good • The Sound of Music.
00311175 P/V/G......................$12.95

Vol. 26 Andrew Lloyd Webber Favorites
All I Ask of You • Amigos Para Siempre • As If We Never Said Goodbye • Everything's Alright • Memory • No Matter What • Tell Me on a Sunday • You Must Love Me.
00311178 P/V/G......................$12.95

Vol. 27 Andrew Lloyd Webber Greats
Any Dream Will Do • Don't Cry for Me Argentina • I Don't Know How to Love Him • The Music of the Night • The Phantom of the Opera • Unexpected Song • Whistle Down the Wind • With One Look.
00311179 P/V/G......................$12.95

Vol. 29 The Beach Boys
Barbara Ann • Be True to Your School • California Girls • Fun, Fun, Fun • Help Me Rhonda • I Get Around • Little Deuce Coupe • Wouldn't It Be Nice.
00311181 P/V/G......................$12.95

Vol. 30 Elton John
Candle in the Wind • Crocodile Rock • Daniel • Goodbye Yellow Brick Road • I Guess That's Why They Call It the Blues • Levon • Sorry Seems to Be the Hardest Word • Your Song.
00311182 P/V/G......................$12.95

Vol. 35 Elvis Presley Hits
Blue Suede Shoes • Can't Help Falling in Love • Don't Be Cruel (To a Heart That's True) • Heartbreak Hotel • I Want You, I Need You, I Love You • It's Now or Never • Love Me • (Let Me Be Your) Teddy Bear.
00311230 P/V/G......................$12.95

Vol. 36 Elvis Presley Greats
All Shook Up • Don't • Jailhouse Rock • Love Me Tender • Loving You • Return to Sender • Too Much • Wooden Heart .
00311231 P/V/G......................$12.95

Disney characters and artwork
© Disney Enterprises, Inc.

FOR MORE INFORMATION, SEE YOUR LOCAL MUSIC DEALER, OR WRITE TO:

HAL•LEONARD® CORPORATION

7777 W. BLUEMOUND RD. P.O. BOX 13819 MILWAUKEE, WI 53213

Visit Hal Leonard Online at **www.halleonard.com**

Prices, contents and availability subject to change without notice.

0605

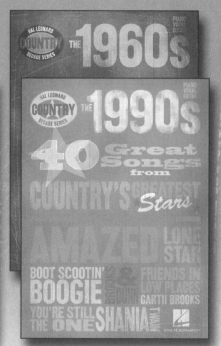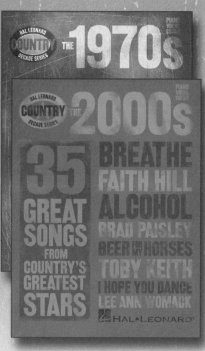